LEARNING MANAGEMENT SCIENCE STRATEGIES

JOHN LOK

Contents

Foreword

Introduction

Any organizations must need management strategy. This book explains how and why organizations ought how to implement effective strategies to help them to set up their businesses more easily in the beginning. Students can understand what our businesses need real requirement in order to implement their businesses more easily and successfully in their business birth stage.

Prologue

Table of content

Chapter 3 Learning organizational communication strategies

Q1 Define the term effective communication p.31-40

Q2 Outline how this case could harm employer-employee relationships in this factory in the future.

Q3 Evaluate the different ways in which Panasonic might communicate any future redundancies to staff and the media.

Chapter 4 Learning Leadership Style

Q1 Explain the types of leadership style Pierre and Oscar most closely represent. p.41-50

Q2 Analyze the possible reasons why Le Menu overspends on food.

Q3 Discuss the advantages and disadvantaged to Le Menu of Oscar's style of leadership.

Chapter 5 Learning organizational behavior

Q1 Explain what you understand by the terms:

a. motivation

b. responsibility

Q2 Identify two factors that seem to influence job satisfaction and explain them in terms of Maslow's hierarchy of needs.

Q3 Explain in terms of the features of job enrichment why it might be easier for small firms to motivate staff than big businesses.

Q4 Discuss the extent to which it might be possible for large firms to use Herzbeng's motivation to improve the level of work motivation. p.51-66

Chapter 6 Learning organizational culture

Q1 Explain on possible reason why Sally thought it necessary to change the organizational culture of Regal Supermarkets.

Q2 Outline the type of culture that Sally seems to be introducing at Regal Supermarkets.

Q3 Analyze the key steps that Sally should have taken to manage cultural change more effectively.

Q4 To what extent will the change in culture guarantee future success for this business? p.67-80

Chapter 7 Learning organizational employee and employee relationship

Q1 Explain what is meant by:

b. collective bargaining

Q2 Analyze two potential benefits to both workers and employees of a globalise union.

Q3 To what extent would any one multinational company be likely to be affected by the development of one large global trade union? p.81-100

Chapter 8 learning crisis management strategies

Q1 Define the following terms:

a. Crisis management

b. contingency plan

Q2 Outline the key steps BP would have gone through to produce a contingency plan for a crisis such as the

Deepwater Horizon.

Q3 Analyze the reasons why the BP share price fell by 50 % following the Deepwater Horizon crisis.

Q4 Discuss the likely benefits and limitations of BP's contingency planning when preparing for any future disasters like Deepwater Horizon.

p.101-120

Chapter 9 Management/Strategic Planning Module

Q1a. Definition of entrepreneur p.121-136

Q1b. Definition of tertiary sector business

Q1c. Definition of finance set up

Q1d. Definition of capital equipment

Q2. Outline of production factors of production needed to set up the business providing to school leavers.

Q3. Business functions of gum instructor's business

Q4. Explain reasons why most enterprisers choose to set up the tertiary sector business

Chapter 10 Partnership definition

Q1 Explains the term of partnership p.137-148

Q2 Outline two benefits to Larry Page and Sergey Brin of starting Google as a partnership.

Q3 Examine the difficulties the partners would have

encountered when they set up Google.

Q4 Explain the term public limited company (plc).

Q5 Discuss the advantages and disadvantages to Google following its conversion to a plc in 2004.

Chapter 11 Cases Strategies Analysis

Q1 Explain the reason for Nike, Inc. having a mission

Q2 Analyze two strategic objectives that Nike, Inc. might try to achieve.

Q3 Using Nike, Inc. as an example, outline the main components you might expect to see in its environment audit.

Q4 Evaluate the advantages and disadvantages to Nike, Inc. of aiming to be a socially responsibility organization.

p.149-160

Chapter 12 Organizational Structure Analysis

Q1 Using examples from the case study, explain the differences between internal and external stakeholders. p.32-43

Q2 Explain the benefits of any two stakeholder groups resulting from this mine project.

Q3 Explain the disadvantages to any two stakeholder groups resulting from this mine project.

Q4 Discuss the ways in which GCM could reduce the impact of the disadvantages it has created for stakeholder groups negatively affected by the mine. p.161-175

Chapter 13 Organization Definition

Q1 Explain the following terms from the text:

1a Public limited company

1b Multinational retailer

1c Technological advances

Q2 Explain how rapid economic growth in China might impact on one aspect of Carrefour's business strategy.

Q3 Analyze the social changes that may be taking place in China which could influence Carrefour's activities in China.

Q4 Produce a PEST analysis for Carrefour as it plans to open new stores in Western China.
p.176-188

Chapter 14 Explaining Strategies Methods

Q1 Produce a SWOT analysis for Four Season Leisure's current position.

Q2a Construct a fully labelled decision tree showing Four Season's options.

Q2b Calculate the expected values for each option.

Q2c On financial grounds state which option Four Seasons should choose.

Q2d Analyse one weakness for Four Seasons of using decision trees as a basis for making
this business decision. p.189-200

Chapter 15 Explaining Business Strategies

Q1 Use the case study to explain the difference between internal and external growth.

Q2 Explain how the business increased sales revenue, yet gained no increase in profits for the

Q3 Assess the likely advantages and disadvantages of a cost leadership strategy for this business.

Q4 Assess the likely advantages and disadvantages of a differentiation or a focused strategy for this business.

p.201-220

Chapter 16 Explaining change management strategies

Q1 define the term change management

Q2 Explain the role a project term might have in changing the direction of HMV.

Q3 Analyze two driving forces and two restraining forces which are influencing HMV's transformation plan as it tries to change the direction of the organization.

Q4 Using an appropriate businesses model, analyse how HMV's proposed takeover of the MAMA Group will give it a competitive advantage in the music industry.

p.221-240

Chapter 17 Explaining international trading management strategies

Q1 Define the term globalisation

Q2 Explain two potential advantages to Kraft of taking over Cadbury

Q3 Analyze the problems Kraft might experience as it tries to enter the European chocolate market.

Q4 Discuss how Ansoff's matrix model might have been useful to Kraft in making the decision to take over Cadbury.

p.241-255

CHAPTER I

Learning human resource management

Q1a. Explain human resource management

This is the strategic approach to the effective management of an organization's workers,

so that who help the business gain a competitive advantage.

Q1b. Explain recruitment

This is the process of identifying the need for a new employee, defining the job to be

filled and the types of staff needed to fill it, attracting suitable candidates for the job and

selecting the best one.

Q1c. Explain part time/temporary contract

A contract is a legal document that sets out the terms and conditions governing an employee's job.

For a temporary contract this is valid for a fixed time period, e.g. six months or one year working

period. For a part time job, this is for less than the normal full working week, e.g. 25 hours out of

a possible 40 full time hours per week.

The hourly paid academic contract is a means of permitting

flexibility in managing the delivery of the academic programme. It allows the college to broaden the scope of teaching by including specialist contributions and more usually, it provides a way of dealing with contingencies, such as unexpected absence or unplanned but temporary increases in workload.

Q2 Explain benefits to college of workplace planning

Workplace planning means this is the establishment of the staff number and skills of the workplace required by the business (college) to meet future objectives. Benefits of workplace planning to college school college management think and plan ahead so that there is time to make major read to strategy if human resources function can't support it.

Efforts to find school staffs, e.g. lecturers, college office administration positions etc. which need select either from outside advertisement or inside staff promotion methods is more suitable for someone is difficult to fill college any positions can be started well in advance.

College can advance to prepare which positions are necessary training, which can be identified and found what are necessary training to get skills to work for identified positions.

During the college decides and exact workforce number for every department is needed, it will not reduce any college staffs. For example, science and geography subject departments won't reduce any lecturers next year if college has working planning to predict how many lecturers are needed in these two subject departments.

Thus, college can take advantage of natural wastage rather than making redundancies which can be costly and

de-motivating and it is bad for college reputation if it often dismiss any staffs suddenly.

What is appropriate for an organization to use depends on how easily it can be implemented and the ease

can be implemented and the ease with which it can be tailored to the situation?

Thus, working planning is long term and takes plan in the context of many other internal and external

influences, so it is not easy to say whether or not it work.

In conclusion, the benefits of conducting workforce planning are that it helps college to get the right people in

the right job of the right time. It allows for a more effective and efficient use of workers and for organizing

to prepare for restructuring, reducing or expanding their reducing or expanding their workforces. In additions,

the process of workforce planning aids organizations by providing objectives which integrate the various units

and allow employees space and time to think about common goals for the future.

Q3 Analyze arguments against offering full time and permanent employment contracts to

the new office staff and lecturers

Full time and permanent employment means a contract is a legal document that sets out the terms and conditions governing an employee's job. For a full time and permanent contract, this is valid for permanent period, but it has probationary period to test the employee whether who has skill and knowledge to do the job. For example, three months or one month probationary period and the normal full working week is a possible 30 hours at least.

Arguments against offering full time and permanent employment contracts to the new office staff and lecturers for college employer. It can be costly to make a permanent full time employee redundant if the business (college) doesn't need them any more and it can not allow greater for changing market flexibility

CHAPTER II

Explaining Human resource culture

Chapter 11 Explaining Human resource culture

Q1 a. Explaining delaying

Delaying means that large organizations flatten their hierarchies. Flattening or delaying, as it is also known

typically elimination of layers in a firm's organizational hierarchy and the broadening of manager's spans

of control.

Q1 b. Explaining cultural conflict

Cultural conflict (differences) also exist in the organizational workplace and impact on human resource

management. When one organization's any department exists different countries staffs who work together,

large organization will have more cultural conflict occurrence between different countries staffs shall

have different personal ideas, education background and working experience and experience to cause

more cultural difference in large organizational departments. Otherwise, small organizations will

exist less cultural conflict because small number of different countries staffs are needed.

Q2 Why cultural conflict seems to exist in Mitsubishi Motors (MMC) Ltd, Japan car maker?

Mitsubishi Motors Ltd reorganises structural Mitsubishi Motors (MMC), the Japanese car maker, it is 37% owned by Daimler Chrysler, revealed significant changes to its senior and middle management structure at a shareholders' meeting. The changes reflected between the company's incoming German managers and established executives who found it difficult adjusting to the new culture.

The restructuring aimed to let some old managers to adapt new management change and other some old managers were to be offered early retirement.

Victoria Emerson, president announced 60 senior staff advisers who were of an advance age and made a marginal contribution to the company despite remuneration would be removed.

Then, she was made chief operation officer appointed a 100 team comprising about 25 mainly non Japanese executives. This team is drawn from different departments, was responsible for overseeing the implementation of the company's restructuring plan.

Some long term service members of Mitsubishi Motors (MMC) Ltd 's middle and upper management resented the presence and power of the company team, all of whom were under 40 years old and who were controlling the strategic direction of it.

The tension between the 100 team (chief operation officer team) and some of MMC 's managers was described as Japanese managers with a job for life attitude. This is not part of German management culture. Thus it will have cultural conflict in possible.

Mitsubishi Motors (Ltd) organizational change emphasizes changes in patterns of behaviour, values, meanings. Thus organizational culture will also change to Mitsubishi culture is often defined as that which is shared by and/or unique to a given organization or group, the social holds together a potentially diverse group organizational members.

Various levels and divisions of Mitsubishi Motors Ltd with have different culture conflict of its organizational hierarchy share a similar viewpoint.

For example, Mitsubishi Motors ltd top executive's commitment is to the value of confronting conflicts and then cited evidence from fiercely argumentative group decision making meetings to demonstrate that Mitsubishi Motors Ltd leaders' values were shared and enacted by power level employees.

Thus, Mitsubishi Motors Ltd cultural change is needed some different countries' staffs will change their culture to adopt any different countries' staffs culture to work together in Mitsubishi staffs culture to work described as Japanese managers with a job for life attitude. This is not part of German management culture. Thus it will have cultural conflict in possible.

Mitsubishi Motors (Ltd) organizational change emphasizes changes in patterns of behaviour, values, meanings. Thus organizational culture will also change to Mitsubishi culture is often defined as that which is shared by and/or unique to a given organization or group, the social holds together a potentially diverse group organizational members.

Various levels and divisions of Mitsubishi Motors Ltd with have different culture conflict of its organizational hierarchy share a similar viewpoint.

For example, Mitsubishi Motors ltd top executive's commitment is to the value of confronting conflicts and then cited evidence from fiercely argumentative group decision making meetings to demonstrate that Mitsubishi Motors Ltd leaders' values were shared and enacted by power level employees.

Thus, Mitsubishi Motors Ltd cultural change is needed some different countries' staffs will change their culture to adopt any different countries' staffs culture to work together in Mitsubishi staffs culture to work together in Mitsubishi Motors Ltd organizations' strategic, business and operative hierarchy levels.

In summary, culture conflict occurs in Mitsubishi Motors Ltd organization because the different countries managers, staffs occupational, educational, working experience background are very different before who choose to work in this company.

Q3 Analyze possible benefits to MMC of reducing the chain of command through delaying.

Benefits of flattening flow primarily from pushing decisions downward to enhance customer and market responsiveness and to improve accountability and morale. Has flattening delivered on its promise to push decisions downward?

Whether Mitsubishi Motors Ltd have delayer and flattened organizational structure can exhibit were control and decision making at the top. The conventional view of flattening, I find that Mitsubishi Motors Ltd CEO eliminated layers in the management ranks, broadened their spans of control and changed pay structures in ways.

CEO and other members of senior management who make resource allocation decisions that ultimately determine Mitsubishi Motors Ltd strategy and performance . Flattening transferred some decision managers to functional managers at the top and flattening is associated with increased CEO involvement with direct reports and the second level of top management .

Corporate structure is as a form of internal governance. Shape how decisions are made and how information is communicated and processed. Another essential element of corporate structure is the compensation scheme that align managerial incentives and guide decision making.

Mitsubishi Motors Ltd hierarchies have changed dramatically. CEO have flattened the hierarchical structure of senior management: they delayer and eliminated management levels and broadened their span of control. Many CEO eliminated the chief operating officer position and increased the number of division managers reporting directly to the CEO. The same CEO also broadened span of control significantly and increase the number of functional managers (e.g. CFO etc) reporting directly to them.

Q4 Discuss possible consequences for efficiency of business of new management structure in Mitsubishi Motors (MML), Japan car maker.

Firms dramatically changes the structure of management compensation by increasing emphasis on performance pay (bonuses, stock options) which is relative to base salaries.

Mitsubishi Motors Ltd is from a multidivisional Japan car maker change to a flattened organization structure firm, increased span structure of control. Multidivisional structure is too much layers and more positions to influence organizational communication.

Mitsubishi motors Ltd has systematically eliminated layers in the hierarchical structure of senior management. Part of this delayer can be attributed to the elimination of key senior management positions.

Thus, possible consequences for efficiency of business of new management structure in Mitsubishi Motors (MML), Japan car maker which include benefits to CEO who has more direct connections deeper in organizations and is potentially more involved in decision making across more organizational units. Thus, division managers‘ decision making is subject to more direct oversight by CEO assigned who exercises more control and pushes decisions up a form of centralization.

Another benefit, it can create organizational knowledge to solve crises which faces easily. For example, one to uncertainty of the future, Japanese Mitsubishi Motors Ltd had to turn to resources outside the organization for new knowledge and insight and the socio-cultural differences between Japan and the western world resulted in their contrasting approaches to knowledge creation.

Tacit knowledge can't be communicated through manuals or theories. Instead , it is knowledge from Mitsubishi Motors maker Ltd' s employees knowledge who gained through experience and knowledge linked to their attitudes and beliefs. individual's ideas are highly value in Japanese Mitsubishi Motor maker Ltd and suggestions and improvements are judged based on Mitsubishi Motor Ltd staffs' merits and is not by the seniority or starting of the individuals in Mitsubishi Motor Ltd.

CHAPTER III

Learning organizational communication strategies

Q1 Define the term effective communication

Effective communication is the exchange of information between people or groups with by written, oral, nonverbal organizational feedback.

Thus, effectiveness communication can help organizations to facility decision making and it can provides information by transmitting the data to identify and evaluate alternative choices, it can provide a release for emotional expression of feelings and is for fulfilment of employees, their work group exchange information with feedback need, it can motivate employees to know what is be done, how well who are doing and what can be done to improve performance.

Q2 Outline how this case could harm employer-employee relationships in this factory in the future.

Panasonic unified communication provides cost effective solutions for small, medium and large business organizations. The solutions combine advanced business telephone products with business clients' user productivity tools, networked directly to standard business application in office.

However, it's organization communicates bad news which

can harm employer -employee relationships in this factory in the future. The cause was the voice at the end of company telephone on 16 Oct. which indicated there would be no redundancies among the 2400 strong work force at the Panasonic factory in Cardiff. But two days later, there would be job cuts, limited to several hundred. On 22 Oct , 1300 people were to be made redundant again. It's handling of the affair was bad management practice.

A manager of human resources is not the appropriate man to announce the bad news to let it's factory workers to know the bad news. Hence, who had not already found another job at the time. It is not fair to them.

Thus, this case could harm employer-employee relationships in this factory in the future as below: It's employee shall lack of trust or management by their employer, it shall cause source of future conflict again, Panasonic management staffs shall lack of respect to their employees for management again, future belief of employee redundancy of rumours could create problems, worker insecurity could result in loss of motivation, trends in low productivity and staff leaving shall increase.

All these factors could harm employer-employee relationships in this factory in the future and in reality a combination of these factors could also harm future relationships between different employees are likely to react in different ways. In fact, the factors could interact and have a cause to effect result in all aspects of Panasonic company efficient and effective operation in the future.

Q3 Evaluate the different ways in which Panasonic might communicate any future redundancies to staff and the media. Refer to all aspects of effective communication, the appropriate sender and receiver, the clarity of the message, the medium to be used and the opportunity for feedback.

Redundancies mean this is job loss due to employee's job no longer being required. This may be because the business re-organizes or because it can no longer afford to employ the employee. Redundancy may be compulsory or voluntary. For legal reasons redundancy needs to be formally stated in a letter, whichever primary method of communication is used. However, I shall evaluate the different ways in which Panasonic might communicate any future redundancies to staff and the media as below:

Suggestion one, group meetings:

Group meeting sender may be a senior UK executive and receivers is groups of workers, e.g. a maximum of 30 worker numbers, the medium is speech and question and answer session, the opportunity for feedback is possible but may be limited.

Meeting advantages include direct questions may be asked and followed up with more questions until full understanding and satisfaction are achieved, the message may be reinforced with caring body language, persuading verbal language speaking used may soften the message and/or be easier to understand. However, meeting disadvantages also include questions may be limited to a few and workers shall lack brave enough to ask questions in front of an audience, time limitation may mean that not all questions are asked, questions thought of after the meeting may not be asked, some workers will have their meeting before others, this can result in incorrect transmission of information and/or the feeling the some workers are considered more important than others.

Suggestion two, One -one-one meetings:

One-on-one meeting sender may be senior department or human resource managers, many managers would be needed to do this for mass redundancies and so the task would need to be split and receiver is each individual worker, the medium is speech and opportunity for feedback is possible but may be limited.

One-on-one meeting advantages include direct questions may be asked and followed up with more questions until full understanding and satisfaction are achieved, every employee can ask the questions which individually concern them, the personal importance of each employee is recognised, the message may be reinforced with caring body language, persuading language used may soften the message and/or be easier to understand.

One-on-one meeting disadvantages include the high stress, face to face situation may be for much for some workers, questions thought of after the meeting may not be asked, some managers may conduct the meeting better than others , special training may be needed in advance and this may cause rumours to spread, some employees have had meeting, so rumours and stress will spread quickly, sequencing of meetings may be different, come employees will have whose meeting before others, which may give the impression that some employees are considered some important than others.

Suggestion three, letter:

Letter sender may be a senior UK executive who is helped by human resource specialists and lawyers, receiver is individual worker, medium is writing, opportunity for feedback is questions could be asked by letter or by requesting a meeting with direct manager or human resource manager. This would need to be stated clearly in the letter.

Letter advantages include for legal reasons, redundancy needs to be formally stated in a letter, whichever primary method communication is used, the wording can be made clear and easy to understand, it is a permanent legal record of redundancy, it can be re-read and thought about carefully over a period of time before questions, questions may be individually asked and answered.

Letter disadvantages include it may seem impersonal to employees who may resent it, especially after long service, letter to a lot of employees may arrive through the postal system on different days, for example, email isn't usually well received and not all employees may have email, email is sometimes not a legally enforceable or valid means of communication, the written interchange of questions are answers

can be very long, the language used may be formal and this may make it seems even more impersonal

and uncaring, so some employees may not understand formal language.

Chapter 4 Learning Leadership Style

Q1 Explain the types of leadership style Pierre and Oscar most closely represent.

The type of leadership style of Oscar partner who represents autocratic style at Le Menu catering business.

Autocratic leadership style features include leader takes all decisions, gives little information to staff,

supervises workers closely, only one way communication and workers only given limited information about

the business.

Oscar is a tough, direct manager, who tells workers exactly what he wants and then expects them always

to meet his high standards. If not, he is quick to let them know; he has a reputation for dismissing temporary

workers part way through an event. Oscar takes the lead during events.

Pierre is much calmer, preferring to consult with his staff. Pierre is more involved with strategy.

Pierre works with Le Menu's chefs on the type of food to prepare for any event.

The type of leadership style of Pierre partner who

represents democratic style at Le menu catering business.

Democratic leadership style features include participation encouraged, two way communication used,

which allows feedback from staff and workers given information about the business to allow full staff

involvement.

Q2 Analyze the possible reasons why Le Menu overspends on food.

The possible reasons why Le Menu overspend on food include the chefs suggest the menu who are not the ones

who control quotes or are responsible for managing the budget, if it employs one costing controller to control

every new menu quotes budget to limit it's overspend, it won't overspend on food in possible;

perhaps most of its food suppliers are expensive to provide food menu for it usually ; quotes may be done by

Oscar partner, whereas it is Pierre partner who works on the menu to do catering operation and management

job in this restaurant. If their communication is poor, the quote and menu may not match; overspends on

food will occur in accident of wrong factors from staffs and these two partners co-operation inefficiently;

quotas are for five course meals with canapes foods and drinks, this may not be fully reflected in the price

because these foods and drinks exclude the other different kind of foods purchase and so who may spend

more than the quoted cost. Owing it decide to buy the other different kind of foods which have not compared

the quotes for the food suppliers before.

Q3 Discuss the advantages and disadvantaged to Le Menu of Oscar's style of leadership.

The advantages to Le Menu of Oscar's style of leadership include as below:

(a) Events are probably high pressure . In these circumstances, one person may need to take urgent decisions for

instant action, as Oscar partner manage this restaurant business by himself who don't need to discuss with

Pierre partner to spend much time to make decision to deal any matters. For example,

Oscar is a direct manager, who tells workers exactly what he wants and then expects them always

to meet his high standards in restaurant.

(b) Temporary staff (new or old staff) are not all experienced in working together and it may need a lot of

firm direction. He has a reputation for dismissing temporary workers part way through an event. Oscar takes the

lead during events. Thus, Oscar partner can help his restaurant to reduce salary to pay to the low cooking skill

of temporary chefs and low service standard of waiters etc staff when he feel their working performance can't

achieve his expectation and he shall dismiss them immediately. For long term, salary expenditure must be

reduced from his management skill.

(c) There will be no question about who is in charge or what to do. Oscar is this restaurant only manager to

let all staff to know who supervise their job and they need to listen their command how to do every job

to achieve whose expectation clearly. So, one to one communication is more easily between Oscar and

his staffs. During another partner Pierre has no authority to control and manage restaurant. Hence,

Oscar partner won't conflict with another partner Pierre often because who doesn't enquire whose opinion how to manage restaurant staffs and operations daily.

(d) Partner Oscar can lead whose waiters service and cooker staffs to co-operate efficiently because who is a direct manager, who tells workers exactly what he wants and then expects them always to meet his high performance standard. Otherwise, he will dismiss them. Thus he must keep the high performance standard of staffs to continue work in his restaurant to raise the reputation of Le Menu restaurant to every clients.

However, Oscar leadership style also has these disadvantages as below:

(a) Oscar's reputation may stop good workers wanting to work for him because who is a direct manager, who need to tell workers exactly what he wants and then expects them always to meet his high standards. If not, he is quick to let them know; he has a reputation for dismissing temporary workers part way through an event. So the quality of service may fall, because who will dismiss his temporary or contract staffs easily when he feels who are not the right staff to do the job.

(b) He may de-motivate workers, leading to lack of enthusiasm or lower productivity and the catering business won't be able to operate if he can't find staffs willing to work for him.

(c) Valuable ideas that come from workers may be ignored from Oscar boss. Thus, this catering restaurant will be difficult to develop to expand its catering service in the future.

(d) Communication channels may be blocked by unwillingness to talk to Oscar boss if his staffs are unwilling to reflect whose ideas to Oscar what who feel need to help when who deal these daily job to feel difficult, it will influence their team co-operation efficiently, e.g. if waiters or chefs teams co-operation can't be efficient, it will cause it's clients need to wait more time to eat and who will feel unhappy to complaint them, even client numbers will decrease during to this reason in the future.

CHAPTER IV

Learning organizational behavior

Q1 Explain what you understand by the terms:

a. motivation

Motivation means the intrinsic and extrinsic factors that stimulate people to take actions that lead to achieving

a goal. Intrinsic motivation comes from satisfaction derived from working on and completing a task. Otherwise,

extrinsic motivation comes from external rewards with working on a task, e. g. payment and other benefits.

b. responsibility

This is the accountability for successful completion of a task /project or achievement of a goal / objective.

It is accompanied by the authority (power) to make decisions , but either carries the bad result of things go

wrong or carries the good result of things go right.

Q2 Identify two factors that seem to influence job satisfaction and explain them in terms of Maslow's

hierarchy of needs.

Maslow's Hierarchy of needs which assumes that what motivates people is unmet needs. According to

Maslow, the needs that motivate people fall into five basic categories:

Physiological needs are the most basic need, physiological needs are the ones required for survival,

then is security needs involve keeping oneself free from harm, next is social needs are the desire for love, friendship and companionship, esteem needs are the need for self esteem and the respect of others,

the final level is the self actualization needs(the highest level need), it describes the desire to live up to

one's full potential. People may be seeking to meet than one category of needs at a time.

These factors that seem to influence job satisfaction: For example, sense of achievement of job satisfaction

and opportunity to develop new skills are belonged to the self actualisation needs level;

recognition of work well done of job satisfaction, e.g. status, responsibility, reward is the esteem needs level;

working in teams/groups with good communication and making workers feel involved of job

satisfaction is the social needs level; contract of employment with job stability of job satisfaction is the

safety needs level; income is from employment of job satisfaction is the physical needs and esteem need

level.

Q3 Explain in terms of the features of job enrichment why it might be easier for small firms to motivate

staff than big businesses.

Job enrichment aims to use the full capabilities of workers by giving them the opportunity to do move

challenging and fulfilling work. It may be easier for small firms to motivate because:

Job enrichment which might be easier for small firms to motivate staff than big businesses, the reasons

include wider responsibilities may be given these are fewer employees to perform tasks.

Large organizations employ many staff, it is more difficult to give them the opportunity to do move challenging and fulfilling work for any staff motivation ; small organizations of each employee may have to fulfil several functions, but large organizations of each employee may more difficult to have to fulfil several functions ; small organizations of full capabilities of each employee may be more personally and individually recognized and used to compare to large organizations of full capabilities of each employee.

Q4 Discuss the extent to which it might be possible for large firms to use Herzbeng's motivation to improve the level of work motivation.

Herzbeng's motivations mean these are factors that results in job satisfaction. They include five match factors as achievement, recognition for achievement, the work itself, responsibility and advancement factors.

It might be possible for large firms to use Herzbeng's motivation to improve the level of work motivation reasons are as employee's achievement is possible as below:

The chance of long term service is as the job uses all of the employee's capabilities fully in large organization is more than small organization; employees' achievement may be recognised by both financial and non financial reward from large firms whose chance is more than small firms. Because large organization can give more chance of financial motivation may include salary or wage increases and bonuses

and chance of non financial motivation may include job enrichment and job enlargement and team working and

empowerment and interest in the work itself can be a significant motivation, e.g. large firms may offer more

scope in technical, scientific or specialist work to whose staff of chance is more than small firms.

Large organizations can have more responsibility to improve the level of work motivation. Responsibility

can be a motivator even it doesn't lead to advancement, e.g. caring, medical, pharmaceutical, law, accounting

etc professional jobs, the large organizational professional staffs need more safety and security feeling

are more than the small organizational professional staffs.

There may be more opportunity for advancement in larger firms through growth (organic or external) and

staff turnover and the fact that large firms usually have many levels of hierarchy through which on

employee can move. Thus, Herzbeng's motivation improves the level of work motivation can use in

large organizations in possible.

However, it also might not be possible for large firms to use Herzbeng's motivation to improve the level of

work motivation as below:

The reasons include that achievement may be limited within the job description, bigger firms have less flexibility, recognition for achievement may be limited as in big firms, the recognition process may be highly bureaucratic and slow. The work itself may be below the aptitude of the workers, e.g. graduates.

Responsibility may be limited to the job description and advancement may be slow to come and there may be a lot of competition for higher position.

Chapter 6 Learning organizational culture

Q1 Explain on possible reason why Sally thought it necessary to change the organizational culture of Regal Supermarkets.

Organizational culture is the values, attitudes and beliefs of people working in an organization that control the way they interact with one another and with external stakeholder groups.

Sally is had experience in the USA as Walmart's chief food buyer who needs to manager this UK largest owned chain of supermarket. In fact, she can't accept this UK Regal supermarket organizational culture so, she uses her USA organizational culture to manage this supermarket.

The possible reason why Sally thought it necessary to change the organizational culture of Regal Supermarkets include that she hoped Regal supermarket can become a highly competitive national marketplace where consumers want low prices and fresh goods to attempt to make more profit, to rise shareholder value after it is sold into a public limited company, to change it's low prices and fresh goods image, to discourage promotion based on long service and loyalty rather than on ability and results.

Q2 Outline the type of culture that Sally seems to be introducing at Regal Supermarkets.

Autocratic leadership style features include leader takes all decisions, gives little information to staff, supervises workers closely, only one way communication and workers only given limited information about the business.

Sally seems to be autocratic leadership style to manage Regal Supermarkets. It includes the following feature:

Power is concentrated among a few people and decisions can be made quickly because there are few people involved in making them because who dismisses 50% of the directors and key managers who had been replaced and staff salary pension scheme was replaced for new recruits with flexible pay and conditions contracts. Staff turnover increased sharply. Thus, managers are judged by result.

Sally tries to adapt the organizational culture of Regal Supermarket business to allow to be successfully in a highly competitive national marketplace where consumers want low prices and fresh foods.

Thus, hierarchical structures are usually typical of power cultures and motivational methods are likely to focus on financial incentives and bonuses for exceptional performance which can encourage

risky and inappropriate decision. These behaviours are an autocratic style leader personal feature.

Q3 Analyze the key steps that Sally should have taken to manage cultural change

more effectively.

Sally had experience in the USA as Walmart's chief food buyer. Currently, she

needed to manage UK Regal Supermarket which is UK one chain of supermarket

stores public limited company. Sally must need to change USA business culture to

accept UK business culture to manage this supermarket. I shall recommend that She should to take

these steps to manage cultural change if who wanted to manage this supermarket more effectively.

Before this UK supermarket organizational culture was like to a big family because Regal supermarkets

has established a culture among its staff that had contributed to its success and growth, loyalty to

family managers was very high, promotion was based on long service and loyalty, customer service

was a priority, it never intended to be the cheapest shop.

But Sally dismissed many directors and key managers, suppliers' terms were shorten, staff salary and

pension scheme was replaced for new recruits with flexible pay and conditions contracts. Staffs turnover

increased sharply. Sally's new organizational management changing will influence the old UK staffs can't accept happily.

Thus, the first step, I recommend Sally needed to enlarge on existing positive aspects of the supermarket business to let these old UK staffs to know why who decided to do these changing and whether what the benefits would give to these old and new staffs in the future. It aimed to make who to get confidence to work continually and who won't choose to work in another supermarkets.

The second step, Sally needed to obtain commitment of people at the top level to assist who to manage any departments in this supermarket business. Otherwise, Sally needed to replace them if they did not give full support.

The third step, Sally needed to establish new objectives and mission statement and she needed to communicate to all staffs and encouraged bottom up communication to let them to know what the future direction is and how Sally hoped her staffs needed to follow organizational policy to do daily jobs efficiently.

The fourth step, Sally needed to train old and new staffs in new methods to adapt new organizational cultural changing.

The final step, Sally needed to change staffs reward system to reward based on new value.

Q4 To what extent will the change in culture guarantee future success for this business?

Sally changes this business old culture, this supermarket

will get these benefits probably as that

higher profitability makes success more likely because Sally plans try to achieve this supermarket

to be successful in a highly competitive national marketplace where consumers want low

prices and fresh goods from another new management cultural methods, emphasis on performance

is more likely to have the business running efficiently because Sally can decide to dismiss any staffs

easily if who feels their performance are not excellent , so staffs will ensure to work carefully,

decisions can be made very quickly when needed because Sally can dismiss directors and key managers

easily who are the top level staffs, so Sally don't need to discuss anyone when who plans to do any matter,

low skilled personal may benefit from autocratic management because whose each salary is also low, Sally

won't choose to dismiss them easily. Otherwise, the high skilled personal , such as managers and directors

who will be dismissed easily because whose each salary is high, so Sally dismisses them to avoid to reduce

more salary expenditure for long term benefit to supermarket.

However, sally's new organizational management culture can not ensure this supermarket will future success

and it is never guaranteed, so Sally ought to bring a USA expert into this UK supermarket who may be

resented because these UK old staffs have been moved from a niche market concentrating on service and family

organizational culture to adapt Sally USA organizational management culture in the future.

Chapter 7 Learning organizational employee and employee relationship

Q1 Explain what is meant by:

a. single union deal (or agreement)

This is an arrangement to an employer recognises only one union for purposes of collective bargaining.

Negotiations may therefore be simplified, as there won't be a diverse range of employee opinions in the

negotiation.

b. collective bargaining

This is the negotiation between employee's representatives (trade unions) and employers and their

representative on issues of common interest such as salary/wage payment and conditions of work. As the

employees are represented as a joint force there is strengths in numbers and individual workers are less

likely to be victimised for standing up for their rights.

Q2 Analyze two potential benefits to both workers and employees of a globalise union.

Swedish journalise Thomas Larsson , in his book "The Race To The Top: The real story of

Globalization (2001), stated that globalization is the process of world distance getting shorter,

things moving closer. It pertains to the increasing ease with which somebody on one side of the

world can interact, to mutual benefit, with somebody on the other side of the world.

The potential benefits to both workers and employees of a globalise union include that:

(a) A globalise union has more powerful collective bargaining power and it gives

globalization of worker rights because trade union leaders are worried by the

growth of globalisation that has weakened their power and reduce their

membership. Because employers can now easily transfer production to low cost countries, the

unions‘ power to bargain and negotiate higher pay deals has been much weakened.

However, a globalise trade union would be able to negotiate with multinationals on behalf of

members throughout the world and this might prevent worker exploitation in very low

wage economies.

It allows negotiation with multinationals to present transfer of production to low cost

countries and exploitation of worker and it stops companies making changes to pay/

rights in one country without consulting workers in other countries.

Thus a globalise union can threaten to global companies (employers) to treat to pay

the unreasonable salaries/wages to whose staffs and workers unfairly.

(b) A globalise trade union challenges the global forces of capital to raise more job opportunities

to different countries workers and employees to get jobs to do more easily because a globalise trade union encourage any local companies to expand to overseas to do multinational businesses.

Thus, one country workers and employees can have more job opportunities to move to another

country to work if the local company expanded to overseas to do multinational company business

and globalise trade union is the middleman role to solve conflicts between any multinational employers and

employees and workers when the employees and workers need it to help any time.

Reference
Thomas Larsson, The Race to the Top: The real story of globalization(US: Cato Institute,
2001), p.9

Q3 To what extent would any one multinational company be likely to be affected by the

development of one large global trade union?

The reasons would be significant for any one multinational company be likely to be affected by the

development of one large global trade union include that
:

(a) One large global trade union could standardise of payment and work conditions, it could lead any one

multinational company to pay higher costs and less competitiveness, therefore a multinational company could

not take so much competitive advantage of cheap labour, which could seriously affect profit.

Any one multinational company could not pay the most minimum labour salaries/wages to its employees in any

countries easily, if one large global trade union developed to standardise of payment and work conditions to protect any countries employees to have the reasonable salaries/wages standard level and improved safe work environment in factories or offices or shops or warehouses working locations etc.

In consequence, any one multinational company would spend more expenditure to labour salaries/wages and any one multinational company also needed to rise expenditure to improve whose working environment to be safety to every employee. Thus, any one multinational company's profit would be reduced largely.

(b) Negotiations may take longer and include a lot more international involvement between any one multinational company and it's employees and workers.

(c) Every country's any one multinational company 's employer and employees issues could also change into a worldwide problem more easily.

(d) One set of negotiations may be a lot simpler than different negotiations in lots of different countries from a globalise trade union.

(e) Any one multinational company acquisition or merger would mean a constant stream of change, which could complicate the whole process and interfere with external growth.

(f) Different local costs of living may be very difficult to take into account for any one multinational company.

(g) A globalise trade union reduces the power of a multinational company over its workforce.

The reasons would also be little or no effect on any one multinational company be likely to be affected by the development of one large global trade union include that :

(a) In practical terms, different local laws and living costs may take the process very difficult to put into effect to any one multinational company because different local law and living costs are external factor to influence to any one multinational company indirectly.

(b) In a recession unions may be happy to have jobs for their workers, so may not take advantage of global negotiating power to any one multinational company directly.

(c) Job losses in one country could lead another new job to another country when any one multinational company does local and overseas business both.

In conclusion, I believe that it is significant for any one multinational company be likely to be affected by the development of one large global trade union. The reason is that multinational firms exist because certain economic conditions make in possible for any one multinational company to profitability undertake production of a product or service in a foreign location. Production of a product or service in foreign market is desirable in the presence of protectionist barriers, high transportation costs, unfavourable currency exchange rate shifts or requirement for local adoption to local demand that make exporting from the

home country unfeasible or unprofitable.

Chapter 8 learning crisis management strategies

Q1 Define the following terms:

a. Crisis management

A crises goes beyond the normal and causes instability or imposes a change in an organization and it can

threaten its future. The impacts of a crisis are therefore experienced across an organization and the

response requires strategic lead in order to (attempt to) manage and control or direction of events.

Thus, a crisis is a form of sudden impact which happens with little or no warning to any organizations.

The origins of a crisis can either be external , where the organization is seen as a victim of an event

beyond its control (e.g. natural disasters) or internal , where a crisis occurs due to accidents in the

workplace (e.g. technical errors) or due to systemic, preventable errors (e.g. human breakdown

accidents, organizational misleads causing injury, or the occurrence of a situation that is

outside the current capacity and experience of the management team, as a result of , for

example, key personnel not being available at a particular point in time).

Crisis management is a term often used to describe the way in which cay organization can handle a crisis.

It is planning relates to get the best position to react to and recover from an emergency, incident reacts

properly and orderly to an incident as it occurs.

Thus, organizations need good crisis management plan to reduce much losses when any crisis occurs.

b. contingency plan

A plan is used by an organization or business unit to respond to a specific systems failure or disruption

of operations.

An organization concentrate on using contingency plan to minimize loss and ensure continuity of the

critical business functions of it in the event of disaster.

It is process of developing advance arrangement and procedures that enable an organization to respond

to an event that could occur by chance or unforeseen circumstances.

Q2 Outline the key steps BP would have gone through to produce a contingency plan

for a crisis such as the Deepwater Horizon.

The British petroleum (BP) company Gulf of Mexico disaster occurred on 20 April , 2010 year, the Deepwater

Horizon drilling rig exploded , killing 11 workers and causing an oil spill that soon became the worst

environmental disaster. If it had produced a contingency plan for any crisis, I believe that the Deepwater

Horizon disaster would not happen easily.

I shall recommend these key steps for it to produce a contingency plan to reduce any business and life loss from

any crisis occurrence in the future as below:

The first step, BP company needs to have strong safety culture. It is the set of values held by employees and it's policies that lead employees to prioritize health, safety and the working environment. Many policies and procedures can affect a Deepwater drilling firm's safety culture and thereby affect employees' actions that could cause a spill. Hence, the top level staffs of chief executive officer and managers to the low level staffs of drilling petrol workers can learn BP safety culture how to work in their working environment safely.

BP can produce a risk analysis to measure all workers whose work environment whether is safe or dangerous in order to permit where their working environment is safe for them to work.

The second step, it needs to produce a crisis communication, it means there are lessons to be learned to all

employees about not only what could have been done to prevent the spill of drilling rig accident occurrence, but about how to combat an environment crisis on the public relations. For example, a crisis response strategy is needed to implemented by the BP on Twitter internet media. It aims to achieve effective in using social media to control the public relations. Crisis that resulted from the explosion and oil spill, people will respond and react on social media outlets. Hence, social media is as a platform to express opinion and attitude in the BP oil spill response and BP can collect more useful crisis handling methods to reduce the disaster of accidents occur again.

The final step, BP needs to provide training to workers to rise their skills to use different equipments and using a compensation structure that encourage individuals to make decisions that increase safety. Upper management ought need to implement internal policies that affect safety culture and makes decisions and lower level managers and other employees respond to incentives created by upper management create a link between safe culture and safe outcomes.

Q3 Analyze the reasons why the BP share price fell by 50 % following the Deepwater Horizon crisis.

After the Deepwater Horizon, explosion disaster occurred on April , 2010 year. It had caused the bad news to BP. The bad news included that BP announced to compensate $20 billion amount to victims of the oil spill and it would not pay every shareholder dividend in 2010 year. Hence, investors would feel it had finance difficult and shareholders felt BP would have loss because who could not receive dividend in 2010 year. It caused it's future shareholders lose confidence to invest to buy its shares, even it's old shareholders would sell their shares immediately. When it's share numbers were decreasing, it would also reduce it's share price fall by 50% seriously.

Q4 Discuss the likely benefits and limitations of BP's contingency planning when preparing for any future disasters like Deepwater Horizon.

The benefits and limitations of BP's contingency planning when prepare for future disaster as below:

The likely benefits of BP's contingency planning can include that:

(a) It will reduce the chance of drilling ring exploding occurrence again.

(b) It will rise the confidence to it's new and old shareholders to continue to invest to it's oil productive business for long term.

(c) It's employees will have confidence to work in its drilling oil rig working environment when who feel their working environment is more safe to work. Otherwise, if it's employees felt who were unsafe to work in its work environment who would leave BP easily , specially, BP's experienced skilful workers would leave BP and found another new employer.

(e) It will build loyalty to public because corporate social responsibility is becoming of great importance and consumers consider more than just its petrol products quality and price when making a purchase.

(f) Understanding exacting how the oil spill was caused and the extent of the damages that resulted, including damages to the natural environment, economy and citizens' health and well being provided evidence as to why people were to dismay by the spill and processing the knowledge that it would have been prevented with some basic safety precaution.

Hence, if it produced a contingency plan, it could give public to have confidence to continue to buy its shares to invest to help it to do business in the future.

However, BP would likely encounter these limitations to implement it's contingency planning as below:

(a) The failure of the America government to assign and in some cases to permit resources to assist with the containment of the oil spill. Although, it can get these benefits from the contingency planning, but it still lacks enough funds to repurchase any advanced and safe oil spill productive equipments.

(b) It needs to spend much time and expenditure to provide training to help it's old and new skilful

workers to learn how to control oil spilling equipments easily to reduce human error and

equipments failure in the short time.

(c) The disaster crisis would have been avoided if proper safe precautions were taken.

For example, reducing drilling Deepwater Horizon to be evacuated overnight to cause

fire occurrence chance to the incident. In fact, BP lacked enough skilful workers and

equipments, so it's workers need to work overnight to cause fire.

In conclusion, BP's contingency planning will likely to get these benefits, but it needs to

have more fund to repurchase many advanced oil spilling equipments and paid more

expenditure to provide training to raise it's skilful workers knowledge to control these

new equipments if it wanted to get the benefits from contingency planning in fact.

CHAPTER V

Management/Strategic Planning Module

Q1a. Definition of entrepreneur

A business is any organization that uses resources to meet the needs of customers by providing a

product or service that they demand. Entrepreneur means an organizer who creates some

new events, organizes factors of production, undertakes risk and handles economic uncertainty

involved in new enterprise/venture. Any entrepreneur has to perform a number of functions

as a vital factor of production.

For example, Jessica wants to start a resume writing service

business who owns these personal characteristics, as hard work, desire for high

achievement, highly optimistic, independence, foresight, good organizer, innovative, time

management, effective communication, analytical ability, independence.

As Jessica is an entrepreneur who may include idea generation and scanning of the best

suitable idea, determination of the business objectives, production analysis and market

research, determination of form of ownership/ organization, raising necessary funds, recruitment, making change and business operation for whose resume writing service.

Q1b. Definition of tertiary sector business

Tertiary sector business activity firms that provide services to consumers and other businesses,

such as retailing, transport, insurance, banking, hotels, tourism and telecommunications, even

including information technological service providers.

Primary sector consists of agriculture, secondary sector is formed by industry and the

tertiary sector is incorporating all other activities that did not fit in first two sectors. For example,

Jessica's business would provide a resume writing service to individuals. Thus, the tertiary sector includes

activities such as trade and domestic activities as well as health, education ,research and development.

The four attributes that are common to service tertiary sector activities include simultaneity

between production and consumption, product intangibility, interactivity between producer and

customer/user and the idea of non-stock.

This characteristics are due to the nature of the services as a work in process, so products are

generated by the tertiary sector which may be tangible or intangible and both physical as well as

information service tertiary sector.

Q1c. Definition of finance set up

Capital consists of finance needed to set up a business any pay. For its continuing operations as

well as the man made resources used in production. These include capital goods, such as computers,

machines, factories, offices and vehicles.

Start up finance means entrepreneur gives whose cash to set up whose business capital

to operate for any business in the beginning. It is sourced either by sole trader or partner's cash or

bank loan or corporation's shares issued capital from shareholders. For example, Jessica buys office

equipments for her resume writing business or gym instructor buys gym sport equipments for

his gym sport service centre business.

Q1d. Definition of capital equipment

Business input of capital equipment is such as computers, machines, printers etc office equipments.

Some firms are capital intensive that is electricity power supply business has a high proportion of capital

equipment to other factors of production . e.g. power station. For example, the gym instructor would

need gym equipments and Jessica needs a computer in office.

Capital equipment presents tangible and fixed assets in any organizations. It means

the tangible items which are to permanently serve the business process. Capital equipment can be

consumed in one accounting period and generally are depreciated over a number of years.

Durable means of production are caused by capital equipment. During its useful life, it gives

off a flow of different usages (e.g. plant equipment). The capital equipment characteristics

include organizational assets are used to supply business operations. Examples include

production line for manufacturing, testing equipment used by a construction company.

Capital equipments are typically high cost, infrequent purchases, that requires good

decision making to minimize long term costs.

Q2. Outline of production factors of production needed to set up the business providing to school leavers.

For this resume writing service to school leavers business of Jessica, its factors of production

may include that the entrepreneur (capital) uses to pay office rent, electricity, water, buying office equipments,

printers and computers and stationary etc general office operational expenditure ; (land) she rents

an office or may work at home to let every school leaver to know where who can give individual working

experiences and educational background information to Jessica to help them to write individual resume;

(labour) Jessica can choose either to work for herself or she can employ employees to assist her.

employing writing resume skilful writers will be intangible asset if who can help her to attract many school

leavers. Instead of employing writing resume assistant, Jessica could also employ cleaner, office receipt,

accounting clerk staffs if she needed.

Finally, the factor of production includes Jessica is a (enterpriser) herself who needs to manage and control

and give ideas how to operate her writing resume service business efficiently and effectively every day.

Q3. Business functions of gum instructor's business

I recommend that gym instructor's gym sport service centre business ought include these departments:

(a) Marketing department can research different gym sport service competitors‘ prices to measure what service fee charging is the most reasonable service fee. It aims to compare their gym sport service quality, the satisfactory level of clients' feeling to play sport bicycles and running machines etc equipment and gym instructor serving attitude to get the most reasonable service fee. Marketing department can design the suitable different payment plans to provide clients to choose payment methods.

After clients use gym sport bicycles and running machines etc equipments from gym instructors instruction, who can choose either to pay service fee per hour or choose to join to be monthly or annual member to pay discount service fee. Thus, I recommend who need to employ at least one market research staff to research the competitors' different service quality and every client satisfaction level to evaluate what is its reasonable price every month.

(b) Finance department can record and analyse his gym business accounting financial information. For example: Purchasing sport bicycles and running machines etc sport centre equipments expenditure, staff salary, rent, electricity, water, insurance etc expenditure.

(c) Human resource department can identify the work force needs, recruits, selects and trains appropriate staff. For example, employing at least one gym service manager gym instructor or gym instructing trainee, cashier, cleaner positions when his business expands.

(d) Customer service department can help every

individual to register member record, cashing, answering enquiry etc front line service in gym sport service centre.

(e) Operating management department can manage gym sport service operation to ensure to satisfy individual need successfully.

Q4. Explain reasons why most enterprisers choose to set up the tertiary sector business

Enterprisers prefer to choose to set up tertiary sector business. The reasons are as below:

Firstly, Developed countries is declining in the importance of secondary sector activity and an increase in the

tertiary sector. It is known as deindustrialisation. Rising incomes associated with higher living standards

have led consumers to spend much of their extra income on services rather than more goods.

These developed countries' people need more entertainment to become their social habits.

Thus, hotel, travel, restaurant, cinema, music, internet etc entertainment tertiary sector businesses

will increase demand in these developed countries.

Secondly, Manufacturing workers may find it different to find employment in other sector of industry and it

causes structural unemployment. Manufacturing businesses in the developed countries face much more

competition and these competitors tend to be more efficient and use cheaper labour. Moreover,

technological innovation causes new technological products import demand increasingly. For example, laptop computers, desk computers, mobiles etc high technological products will increase demand because developed

countries' people have afford money to buy these products commonly. It rises import and domestic secondary

sector firms have been forced to close.

Thirdly, enterprisers don't require large amounts of capital to buy capital equipments if who choose to

do tertiary sector service or trading businesses.

Finally, some enterprisers rely on their past tertiary sector business experience own skills and interest.

Thus, It implies entrepreneurs have more opportunities to choose to set up service or trading tertiary sector

businesses in any developed countries market nowadays.

CHAPTER VI

Partnership definition

Q1 Explains the term of partnership

A partnership is a collaborative relationship between two or more people to work toward shared objectives

through a mutually agreed division of labour. Partners can deliver of practical solutions at the strategic level

to carry on business together, with shared capital investment and usually shared responsibilities.

The characteristics of partnership include a shared leadership among individuals who are empowered

by own organizations and trusted by partners to resolve conflicts, a shared common vision and purpose

that recognizes value contribution of all members and acceptance of differences (e.g. values, ways of

working) is key components of a successful partnership.

Q2 Outline two benefits to Larry Page and Sergey Brin of starting Google as a partnership.

The two benefits to Larry Page and Sergey Brin of starting Google as a partnership include these

two hands.

They can exchange their individuals with networking skills, sharing information, coordinating efforts,

transferred or combined service and governance and resources to concentrate on managing themselves

internet commerce field to operate partnership together. Hence, they can achieve strategic alliance benefit of decision making power is shared or transferred. Management of a program or mutual interest to participating organizations' missions to reduce risk by one internet technological firm itself.

The another hand, their business losses can shared and additional capital can injected by each partner to have enough capital to expand their internet technological business in the short term.

Q3 Examine the difficulties the partners would have encountered when they set up Google.

The difficulties the partners would have encountered when they set up Google which can include these two factors of external competitive environment and internal organization cooperation factors.

On the internal organization cooperation factor, they can exist different vision and ideas to operate whether one partner dominates or partners compete for the lead, lack of understanding role and responsibilities and lack of support from partner organizations with decision making power and difference of philosophies and manners of working and lack of commitment and unwilling participants and financial and time commitment outweigh potential benefits and too little time for effective consultation and spending much time to get trust to build long term partnership relationship and employees need time to adapt new organizational culture and change management between of them during they set up Google in the beginning together.

For example problems include that design company logo and administration and managing employee

cooperation and deciding what users are looking for from their websites and how to calculate page's room

housed in their servers and how to make users spend as little time as possible on their website search etc

problems. When they set up Google internet technological business in the beginning.

On the external competitive environment factor, it faced the Yahoo internet technological monopoly.

It provided email service, news headlines, a website directory, advertisement, webpage hosting and

other online services to different countries. Yahoo sources of revenue include sale of

advertisement space, paid premium, content and extended service commission for sale made through

its online stores and park link placement. Hence, these two partners set up partnership which need have

unique internet service to win their this Yahoo competitor in this internet commerce market in the beginning.

Q4 Explain the term public limited company (plc).

Public limited company is incorporated legal form of organization to run business. Companies are

incorporated to form an entity with a separate legal personality. This means that the organization can do

business and enter into contracts in its own name.

A public limited company is owned by its members (shareholders), who have invested in the business and

enjoy limited liability. For example, the company's finances are separate from the personal finances of owners.

It has legal right to sell shares to the general public. Its shard price is quoted on the national stock exchange.

Q5 Discuss the advantages and disadvantages to Google following its conversion to a plc in 2004.

Although, Google changed to public limited company form from partnership in 2004 and it's revenue

sources must not be changed after 2004. Generally, Google drives its revenue for two sources: Sale of its

research technology to other companies and sale of advertisement space on its search result pages.

However, it will still have advantages and disadvantages to a public limited company in 2004.

It's advantages include it was a partnership and it can't issue shares to public to increase capital before. After

2004, it formed a public limited company, it can ease of buying and selling of shares for shareholders to

encourage investment and access to substantial capital sources due to the ability to issue a prospectus to the

public and to offer shares for sale, public limited company can have separate legal entity and limited liability to

Google.

Otherwise, public limited company also have these disadvantages include it needs legal formalities in

formation, cost of business consultants and financial advisers when creating it, share prices subject to

fluctuation, sometimes for seasons beyond business's control from poor economy, legal requirements

concerning disclosure of information to shareholders and the public, e.g. annual publication of detailed report and accounts, risk of takeover due to the availability of the shares on the stock exchange and directors

are influenced by short-term objectives of major investors.

CHAPTER VII

Cases Strategies Analysis

Q1 Explain the reason for Nike, Inc. having a mission

A mission statement is a statement of the organization's purpose, what it wants to accomplish in the larger environment.

The reasons for Nike , Inc needs a mission statement as below:

(a) Nike, Inc. is a sport products trading company. it needs have a clear mission statement because

Nike, Inc. can know what it's business is, who it's clients are, what clients value do and what it's

business should be these questions to achieve its business intention more successful if it had a clear mission

statement . Thus, its stakeholders can know core purpose and activity in a short paragraph.

For example, it's mission statement is to bring inspiration and innovation to every athlete in the world of

whose every body and who can become athlete successfully.

(b) The reason for it needs have a mission statement include it can give message to let Nike's clients and

employees to know what it's products can attribute in global sport product market, it should be translated into

supporting objectives for each level management and create a hierarchy of objectives that are consistent with

one another within organization, Nike's objectives are followed the mission statement. All mission statement can influence it's objective can be achieved. Thus, it can recognise the markets and benefits of serving these sport markets.

(c) It can give ethical reference to motivate employees by identifying positive core goals.

Q2 Analyze two strategic objectives that Nike, Inc. might try to achieve.

Nike, Inc was formed as an importer of Japanese shoes, 1962. Today, Nike was holding a global market share of approximately 37% (Puma.com) In the United States, it's sport products were sold through about 22,000 retail accounts; world wide, it's products were sold in more than 160 countries. It developed to sell of athletic footwear, apparel and equipment, which together approximately $18,6 million in sales during Nike's 2008 year. It divided its products into four segments: footwear, apparel, sport equipment and other products. In 2008, these segments accounted for 52%, 28%, 6% and 14% of Nike's revenue respectively (Adidas Group.com). In addition to manufacturing sportswear and equipment, it operated retails stores the Nike town name. Nike's competitors, like New Balance, but also against large athletic footwear and manufacture like Adidas AG and Puma. Thus it implied Nike had good strategic planning to achieve it's sale objective before.

However, I think Nike should have these problems which would encounter in the future. For example, although Nike always represents high quality and highly reliable. However, the cost will be higher than other brands. The public feels that Nike overcharges its consumers and should reduce the price of their products

and it had any new sport products to develop because clients' taste are varied from time to time and it's

sport products' life cycle are getting short and clients can have a wide range of selection from running

shoes or sunglasses with Nike brand in the future and fake products could be one of the most critical

reasons for Nike. In fact, in some Asia countries: Taiwan, China or Vietnam. Nike could lose more than

million dollars because they don't have effective way to stop those take products.

There should be specific , measurable, achievable, realistic and time specific and should be based on the

corporate aims.

However, I shall recommend these two strategic objective that Nike, Inc. might try to achieve.

Strategic planning means the process of developing and maintaining a strategic fit between the

organization's goals and capabilities and its changing marketing opportunities.

The first strategic objective , it can raise sales by 5% by end of the year. It's methods can include that

Nike might try to analyze it's current business portfolio of sport running shoes and sport equipments etc

products to judge different countries' clients' number of age group segments to buy their different product

numbers in the future. This strategic objectives is to create value for Nike Inc. clients and build clients

relationship by market segmentation and targeting.

Hence, on the strategic level, Nike Inc. might design business portfolio in its strategy. Business portfolio

is the collection of businesses and products that make up it. Thus, Nike Inc. must analyze its

current business portfolio or strategic business units and decide which strategic business units

should receive more or less or should downsize its business portfolio by eliminating some style of

sport running shoes and equipment etc products designs of business units that are not profitable

or that no longer fit Nike's overall strategy.

Another method include that differentiation is creating superior customer value by actually differentiating the

market offering and positioning is arranging for a product to occupy a clear, distinctive and desirable place

relative to competing products in the minds of target consumers.

Nike might try to diversify to produce more new style and design sport running shoes and new sport

equipments product numbers to attract more clients to choose to buy its sport products. This market strategy is

differentiation and positioning in global sport product markets, aim to win its competitors. For example: Old

styles in new colour athletic running shoes.

The another strategic objective, Nike can achieve all new sport products developed during the year

should use materials from natural sources and it can carry out an environmental audit of the sport

product range by the end of the year.

Its methods can include that Nike can cut greenhouse gas emissions by 10% in all factories by the end

of year and all new sport products developed during the year should use materials from natural sources or renewable resources and use suppliers who are socially responsible and implementation of the common

high standards for the wellbeing of all employees. For example, giving fair salary to factories workers,

willingness to pay cost of environment protection and establishment and implementation of ethical codes

of practice to become a socially responsible organization.

Reference

Financial reports (2009), PUMA.com, http://about.puma.com/EN/5/35/35/.

Income statement (2009), Adidas Group, http;//adidas-group.corporate-publications.com/en/group-management-report/income-statement-7.html.

Q3 Using Nike, Inc. as an example, outline the main components you might expect to see in its environment audit.

Nike, Inc.'s factories need have safety and clean working environment for their workers to work

and reduce air and water pollution to natural environment from its plastic wastage to

damage natural environment to influence different countries stakeholders of citizen health.

Its plastic wastage pollution level is very serious to influence the manufacturing countries

stakeholders of citizen health daily. Hence, its environment audit needs outline these main components

as below:

. Use of renewable resources to make the sport products.

. Implementation of common high standards for the wellbeing of all employees.

. use suppliers who are socially responsible.

. Implementation of long term socially responsible aim rather than short term profit objectives.

. Willingness to pay cost of environmental protection.

. Establishment and implementation of ethical codes of practice to become a socially responsible organization.

Q4 Evaluate the advantages and disadvantages to Nike, Inc. of aiming to be a socially responsibility organization.

Nike, Inc needs to be a socially responsibility organization to concern its stakeholders of consumers,

employees, environment benefit. Nike, Inc was a organization to become more increasing global,

it is becoming more difficult to ensure ethical to supply chain and takes on ethical approach to

managing the workplace that extends beyond organizational national and cultural boundaries.

For example, Nike, Inc. has strong research and development apartments is because Nike's sport products are

manufactured in low wage factories in the far East countries. Therefore they can concentrate on

marketing image and research project. However, it's low salary workers need have human right

protection to rise their reasonable wage level. Thus it is not a socially responsibility organization, it

needs to implement a socially responsibility organization to make stakeholders to believe in the future.

However, it will have advantages and disadvantages during it plan to achieve a social responsibility

organization.

On advantages hand, it can promote good public image, it is pride of employees can be a motivator, it is being ahead of changes in law which can give time to find cheaper solution and it can avoid

costly bad media publicity on damaging natural environment issues.

On the disadvantages hand, it needs to increase cost to produce new sport products, it needs to take

manpower and attention from other important aims and objectives, it's result will be long teem rather than

short term, stakeholders will be conflict on socially responsible and ethical issues and it is possible that

it will drop in profit due to increase costs and may have negative effect on share prices.

CHAPTER VIII

Organizational Structure Analysis

Chapter four Organizational Structure Analysis

Q1 Using examples from the case study, explain the differences between internal and external stakeholders.

Stakeholders are groups of people or individual who can be affected or is affected to gain advantages or

disadvantages by the achievement of purpose and action taken by an organization. Stakeholders can be

individuals, communities, social groups organizations. For example, stakeholders in a forest policy might

include people who live in or near the relevant forests, people who live further away who live further

away who use those forests, settlers from where in the country or abroad.

British GCM Co does mining/coal project scheme in Bangladesh country.

It's internal stakeholders are people who own or work for it's mining/coal project in Bangladesh country. For

example, shareholders, managers, workers, directors etc all staffs.

It's external stakeholders are people who do not work for or own a business for it's mining/coal

project scheme in Bangladesh country. For example, Bangladesh country Government, the world development

movement organization, the Asian development bank loan lender, local residents, international campaign groups, local newspapers and TV channels, local farmers and landowners etc.

Q2 Explain the benefits of any two stakeholder groups resulting from this mine project.

Stakeholders group have benefits from GCM Co mine project scheme in Bangladesh country which include GCM employees, GCM shareholders, landowners, Asian development bank, suppliers etc.

GCM Co needs invest large expansion of its coal/mining business project by building a new head office and coal/mine site to develop natural resource in Bangladesh country.

Possible benefits impact on Bangladesh country central and/or local Government which larger new head office will lead to increase payments to Bangladesh country local Government through local business taxation , a mining project would provide a boost to the Bangladesh country economy, a lot of tonnes of coal would be exported, it brings a valuable foreign currency for the economy. The mine/coal could also supply cheap coal for power generation in Bangladesh country providing a cheap source of electricity and further boosting the economy. Jobs would also be created, helping the Government to achieve its macro economies objectives as well as local community, the mine project would employment and a some of income to members of the local population. This income will be spent on local services and goods, further benefiting the local community.

Possible benefits impact on Bangladesh country suppliers of information technology to provide service to

GCM Co to help them to earn more income because it needs new information technology coal/mine productive machines to rise coal workers efficiency and shorten time to produce coal production. It may lead to reduce mining/coal nature waste to produce more coal/mining natural resource from information technological machines. Thus, it can raise to sell more coal/mining numbers from high information technological machines to earn more profit to shareholders.

Q3 Explain the disadvantages to any two stakeholder groups resulting from this mine project.

The mine/coal project needs much lands physically and economically displace many people. This displacement will take place in one of the most densely populated countries in the world and will destroy a critical agricultural region in the Bangladesh country.

It will cause disadvantages to local community, the environmental damage is caused by mining, it would be indicated by land development movement. The mining would spoil landscape and cause diversion of a river and destruction of a forest, will resulting impact on those who depend on the forest for making living. For example, farmers and local community homes would have to be relocated.

It will cause disadvantages to it's employees, the mining/coal project may being employees into conflict with the local community and who are against the mine/coal job. Although workers need the work, who may feel uncomfortable about the significant destruction of environment being caused by the mining/ coal

project.

Q4 Discuss the ways in which GCM could reduce the impact of the disadvantages it has created for stakeholder groups negatively affected by the mine.

GCM co can reduce impact of disadvantages , it has created for stakeholder groups negatively affected

by mining/coal project scheme in Bangladesh country.

They include that workers whose homes are moved, so GCM Co can offer compensation and it can build better

home for them, landowners who have land forcibly purchased, so GCM Co can offer more than the current

market price and arrange meetings to explain that they will be compensated, farmers whose land now has no

water due to relocated river, so GCM Co can offer compensation and/or jobs in the new mining/coal to

family members.

CHAPTER IX

Organization Definition

Q1 Explain the following terms from the text:

1a Public limited company

Public limited company means an incorporated limited liability business whose shares are traded

publicly on the stock exchange and whose reports and accounts are publicly available.

1b Multinational retailer

This is a chain of shops that operates in various countries in addition to the country in which its

headquarters is located.

1c Technological advances

These are innovations in machinery, equipment or computer systems which may allow the

business to improve efficiency of operation and /or economies of scale.

Q2 Explain how rapid economic growth in China might impact on one aspect of Carrefour's business

strategy.

Business planning is a management-directed process of identifying long-term goals for a business or

business segment, and formulating realistic strategies for reaching those goals. Through planning,

HYPERLINK "http://www.referenceforbusiness.com/encyclopedia/Kor-Man/Management.html" management decides what objectives to pursue during a future period, and what actions to undertake

to achieve those objectives.

Carrefour was the world's first department store opened in Paris, France in 1959. Although it didn't

enter China market unteil 1995, the speed of its development in China has been faster than any other

countried. To June of 2006, Carrefour had established 78 chain stores in China, starting with

first store in Beijing, Carrefour arrived in Shanghai and Shenzhen in 1996.

Carrefour developed so rapidly in China because China can offer it very good economic benefit

and development of Carrefour in China has realized economies of scale. Thus, Carrefour one aspect of

business strategy is to such as the establishment of distribution centres to reduce transport and

distribution costs to expand more supermarket in China different cities.

For example, Carrefour's supermarkets have established special counters for quality line foods.

They havea clear brand logo, foods are packaged, not only quality line label, but also with supplier

information on a traceable barcode. The quality line is control and supervision by Carrefour raw

and freash agribulture food throughout the supply chain from planting and processing to distribution,

in order to guarantee the quality and safety of foods of Carrefour own brand.

The quality line has a number a key aims to maintain traceability throughout the supply chain from planting to eating, to produce agriculture food with no pesticide reside, to ensure quality is consistent

and reliable, to use environment friendly production and processing technologoes and produce

at a price acceptable to market to be lower than truly organic food because only a few consumers can

afford organiz food.

It decentralized management. It divided its Chinese to structure into four regions of East China,

South China, North China and middle China. It used local partners, such as Shanghainese partner

in Shanghai, a Cantonese partner in Guangzhou and a Beijing partner in Beijing.

It also employed China storemanagers to manage it's supermarkets, their duties include foods on

orders, purchasing, pricing supplier selection, arrangement and store displays, employees

recruitment and negotiating promotional campaigns etc. Employing foreign Chineses to manage

its supermarkets in China is more acceptable to it local clients in China.

Moreover, Carrefour has a variety of cooperative ways of working with agriculture food

suppliers in China by joint operation. Thus, Carrefour business strategy competes against its

supermarket competitors on the basic of price, convenience and customer experience.

In conclusion, this business strategy is such as the establishment of distribution centres in China, it achieved Carrefour could expanded established 78 chain stores in China in 2006.

Q3 Analyze the social changes that may be taking place in China which could influence Carrefour's

activities in China.

Since the mid-1990 year, changes have taken place in consumers' demands for agriculture food in

China, citizen's incomes have increased rapidly, rapid growth of Gross domestic product per capita.

People's food demands have changed from quantity to quality, safety and diversity, rise in education levels

and improvement in social welfare and improved communication with other countries.

The first supermarkets were developed rapidly in China from 1990 and China's entry into the world

trading to begin to open its retail market in general and in 2004 foreign businesses entered China's market and

the increasing competition among and between supermarkets and traditional retail stores.

China consumers traditionally buy raw and fresh agriculture food every day. So the quality and availability

of raw and fresh agriculture food has become an important measurement of supermarkets' attractiveness

to clients. Many supermarkets provide organic and green agriculture foods in their stores too (Hu, D. 2005).

Because China economic growth to cause social changes, it could influence Carrefour

carried on these activities sell its agriculture foods in its China supermarkets as below:

Although economic development and improvement in people's living standards, China customers demand the quality of raw and fresh agriculture food and choice of varieties and safety agriculture food in China are rising. Thus, Carrefour classifies these raw and fresh agriculture food into five categories: Fish, meat, fruit and vegetables, salads and breads. Carrefour must keep these foods to save in clean and cold store room to keep all foods to be fresh to prepare to sell to it's clients from Fresh transportation process.

China social changes cause it has many diverse cultures and consumers. For example, Beijing drink beer social changes adapt to local tastes and preferences in these areas. Carrefour introduces new products, such as wine to China and promotes wine fairs and educates Chinese how to drink wine and what foods it goes with. Carrefour imports wine to Chinese to adapt to local taste or by using its knowledge from Taiwan.

Carrefour's selling strategies also be changed to adapt to sell fish alive and sell frozen fish to the China bigger cities preferred to buy fish alive, right out of fish tanks. Chinese west and middle China preferred to purchase frozen fish because they are further away from the coast and want fish to be fresh. Thus China social changes also change Carrefour's fish sale behaviour in China supermarkets to adapt to local consumer and shopping behaviours.

Rising Asian middle class and China consumers are more conscience of health and environment and Carrefour can have its own line of organic foods and it stocks fair trade products and it has also reduced energy

energy consumption and disposable plastic bag numbers in China is a opportunity to Carrefour to do food sale

business.

In conclusion, China social changes brought Chinese consumers like to compare different brands. Thus,

Carrefour must introduce larger shelves in order to place all different brands in one areas in supermarkets.

Reference

Hu, Dinghuan (2005), On the binary structure of agriculture food: The impact of supermarket development

on the agriculture sector and agriculture food safety, Chinese Rural Economy, no.2 pp.12-17.

Q4 Produce a PEST analysis for Carrefour as it plans to open new stores in Western China.

PEST analysis elements include political, economic, social and technological aspects.

As Carrefour plans to open new stores in Western China. It needs to produce a PEST analysis to help it

to know China external environments factors to affect it's business objective and strategies to achieve

its business aim in China supermarket market successfully.

On the political aspect, China opens world trading market to let different countries investors to establish

their businesses in Western China. This Carrefour can enter China supermarket market more easily.

On the economic aspect, the current devaluation of the Euro will import more expensive to European businesses. This is a threat to Carrefour to enter western market, Rising Asian middle class in Western China can increase supermarket food purchase demand.

On the social aspect, Western China consumers are more conscience of health and environment and Carrefour can have its own line of organic foods and it stocks fair trade products and it has also reduced energy energy consumption and disposable plastic bag numbers in Western China. It is a opportunity to Carrefour to do supermarket business in Western China.

On the technological aspect, social networking sites provide an opportunity for Carrefour supermarket because which can be used to increase customer loyalty to brand, e.g. twitter and face book can be used to create commonly for loyal of Carrefour's clients in Western China easily.

Chapter six Explaining Strategies Methods

Q1 Produce a SWOT analysis for Four Season Leisure's current position.

A SWOT analysis is a form of strategic analysis that identifies and analyses the internal strengths and weaknesses and external opportunities and threats that will influence the future direction and success of a business. Thus, a SWOT analysis provides information that can be helpful in matching the firm's resources and strengths to the competitive environment in which it operates. It is useful in strategy formation and selection.

Four Season Leisure's SWOT analysis for current position as below:

Internal strengths: Thirty years of providing holidays to high income European and North American consumers travel business experiences to build most famous brands in the Caribbean, it has attributed the group's relative success to effective management from a team of people that have considerable knowledge and expertise in the travel market.

Internal Weaknesses: It's concentration in the Caribbean travel market is weakness.

External opportunities: The world economic slow down and it causes traveller demands decrease, expanding into some of the new destinations that its customers are interested in visiting.

External threats: Increasing Four Season Leisure's share of the travel market, all inclusive holiday resort market, The competition is from new holiday destination such as Dubai.

Q2a Construct a fully labelled decision tree showing Four Season's options.

Four Season's decision tree economic conditionsinitial cost projected profit
expected value
Option 1: Open new resort ($120 million) fast growth $40 million x20%
in Dubai

normal growth $200 million x 50%

recession -($100 million x 30%)

Option 2: Open new resort

in Thailand ($150 million) fast growth $500 million x 20%

normal growth $300 million x 50%

recession -($50 million x 30%)

Option 3: Upgrade existing ($80 million) fast growth $150 million x 20%

existing resorts

in Caribbean normal growth $120 million x 50%

recession -(%100 million x 30%)

Q2b Calculate the expected values for each option.

Four Season leisure expected values as below:

Option 1

fast growth $40 million x20% + normal growth $200 million x 50% - recession ($100 million x 30%)

Thus option 1 expected value is $78 million

Option 2

fast growth $500 million x 20% + normal growth $300 million x 50% - recession ($50 million x 30%)

Thus option 2 expected value is $235 million

Option 3

fast growth $150 million x 20% + normal growth $120 million x 50% - recession ($100 million x 30%)

Thus option 3 expected value is $ 60 million

Q2c On financial grounds state which option Four Seasons should choose.

Four Season Leisure will choose option 2 because it's expected value is $ 235 million and it's economic condition initial cost is $150 million, it can earn predict profit is $85 million.

However, the other two options is both initial cost amount is much than expected value

, so it have predicted loss.

Q2d Analyse one weakness for Four Seasons of using decision trees as a basis for making
this business decision.

Decision trees is a technique that considers the value of the options available and the chance

of them occurring. It is a diagram that sets out the options connected with a decision and the

outcomes and economic returns that may result.

Four Season leisure uses decision trees to make business decision to predict which travel

destination option can earn the largest expect value, if it evaluates the fast growth,

normal growth and recession occurrence chance is wrong, it will choose the expect value

is not the nest financial return. Thus decision trees has possible the incorrect fast growth,

normal growth and recession to predict for these travel destination expect value.

CHAPTER X

Explaining organizational strategies

Chapter seven Explaining organizational strategies

Q1 Use the case study to explain the difference between internal and external growth.

Traffic clothing plc produces suits and dresses and sells them to major retailers in several

countries. It plan to grow it's clothing manufacturing business to overseas.

Internal growth can be achieved in a number of ways and these forms of growth can lead

to differing effects on stakeholder groups, such as customers, workers and competitors.

Reasons include to plan these internal growth strategy of sale turnover have grown

by around 15% each year, but a slower rate than some competitors, aims to increase

much profit. For example, Traffic clothing plc plans to open own clothing retailer

shops in towns and cities to offer customers a top quality shopping experience to allow

suits and dresses differentiation in a crowded markets , aims to increase market

share in clothing industry. Increased economic of scale of internal growth strategy,

traffic low prices have been possible due to the opening of low cost factories in

developing countries.

External growth means business expansion is achieved by means of merging with or

taking over another business from either the same or a different industry.

It's external growth strategy could be achieved by aggressive takeover either other

clothing producers or material suppliers to achieve cost leadership, it would focused on a

small, higher in come market segment in several overseas markets.

This could be reinforced with a merger with a prestige clothing retailer.

Q2 Explain how the business increased sales revenue, yet gained no increase in profits for the last three years.

Traffic clothing plc can increased sale revenue by around 15% each year, yet gained to increase in

profits for the last three years.

The reasons include these factors, new competitors were entering the clothing market and driving down

prices, raw material prices for both natural and man-made inputs were rising, the number of merger between

large clothing retailers had increased that bargaining power when dealing with producers like Traffic.

Q3 Assess the likely advantages and disadvantages of a cost leadership strategy for this business.

The advantages and disadvantages of a cost leadership strategy for Traffic clothing plc manufacturing

business as below:

Cost leadership strategy means the lowest cost producer in the industry for a certain level of product

quality will allow the firm to make higher profits than competitors or if the businessman lowers its prices below the average of competitors, to increase market share. This strategy usually targets a broad rather than a niche market, e.g. Ryanair, one of Europe's largest and most profitable airlines, is also the lowest average cost airline. Thus, traffic clothing plc adapts this cost leadership strategy either producers suits and dresses due to opening of low cost factories in developing countries to sell to major retailers in several countries at average industry prices to earn higher profit than clothing competitors or below industry average prices to gain market share.

The cost leadership advantages to Traffic clothing plc include that it can spend more extra money to invest to buy of high level of advanced clothing production machines to shorten time of the clothing manufacturing process in efficient production methods for rise to produce many suits and dresses numbers to sell to major retailers in several countries, economic of scale to produce suits and dresses to reduce clothing manufacturing cost for long time.

However, cost leadership strategy also has these disadvantages to Traffic clothing plc includes that it could be achieved b aggressive takeover of either other clothing producers or material suppliers to achieve cost leadership if it expanded its clothing manufacturing business by means of merging to them to taking one another business from either the clothing manufacturing industry or clothing retail industry.

Thus, it would give cost leadership benefits to it's competitors in clothing manufacturers or clothing retailers.

Q4 Assess the likely advantages and disadvantages of a differentiation or a focused strategy for this business.

The advantages and disadvantages of a differentiation or a focused strategy for Traffic clothing plc as below:

Differentiation strategy advantages involves developing a product or service that offers unique features valued

clients.

Traffic clothing plc can own clothing retail shops in itself and several countries to offer customers a

top quality shopping experience, this will allow differentiation in a crowed market.

Traffic clothing plc can rise suits and dresses sale value added to its clothing product or provide training

to raise sale people service performance by these features may allow it to charge a premium price for it

when it's clients feel a top quality shopping experience from its sale people service performance. It can

help strong sales team able to promote the perceived strengths of its brand and its suits and dresses clothing

products, rising Traffic clothing plc corporate reputation for innovation and quality and it can have extra

money to prepare excellent research and development clothing manufacturing machine facilities.

However, differentiation strategy has disadvantages to it, it needs spend much money to invest

to buy high speed and advanced clothing manufacturing technological machines to help it to rise to

produce high quality and unique of suits and dresses clothing products in the short time and it needs to lend loan from banks if it has no enough capital to buy these clothing manufacturing machines.

The focused strategy concentrates on a narrow market segment, aiming to achieve either a cost advantages or differentiation. This can lead to a high degree of customer loyalty within the market segment.

Traffic clothing plc focused strategy could be achieved by aggressive takeovers of either other clothing producers or material suppliers to achieve cost leadership, focusing on a smaller, higher income market segment. This could be reinforced with a merger with a prestige clothing retailer.

Advantages include Traffic clothing plc can concentrate on sell its suits and dresses clothing products to several countries, eg. young age between 20 to 40 male or female group clients.

However, disadvantages include, it needs to time to gather information about it's client age target to choose which major several countries and the young age group in different countries of clients .

If it's clothing sale numbers reduced, even it will have too many old clothing stocks to keep in its warehouse, it has no power to sell these old clothing stocks for long time.

These old clothing stocks would be obsolete, it's clients won't willing to accept to buy old style clothing or damaged clothing in warehouse to keep long time.

CHAPTER XI

Explaining change management strategies

Q1 define the term change management

Change management involves planning, implementing, controlling, and reviewing the movement

of an organization from its current state to a new one.

The change management includes external and internal factors. Planned change results from deliberate

decisions to alter an organization and unplanned change is imposed on the organization and is often

unforeseen.

Internal forces for change include things like declining effectiveness (resignations or major accidents),

changes in employee expectations and changes in the work climate, e.g. organizations need to develop

and improve reasons.

External forces for change include globalization, workforce diversity, technological innovation,

ethics. Change may take one of three forms, incremental change is relatively small in scope and as such,

results in small improvements. Strategic change is a larger scale approach that is similar to a restructuring

effort.

Thus, change management moves the organization forward a different and sometimes, unknown future state.

Q2 Explain the role a project term might have in changing the direction of HMV.

Change management is a complex and large subject area which tends to form part of higher level questions.

Project team means a group of employees entrusted with managing a defined project (this may be a change

management project). The team may consist of special employees required from the success of the

new project.

Thus HMV music entertainment business project team role and responsibilities may include:

Identification of areas of change, e.g. changing by acquisition, pure MHV loyalty card scheme, 50%

stake in 7 digital, pilot HMV (Urzon -branded cinema in Wimbledon), establishment of new vision

and objectivity to design new organization management structure to adapt new management structure

after HMV music entertainment business takeovers HAMA Group, ensuring resources are enough to used

in planning change, e.g. timing, legal, marketing development etc requiring, implementing and controlling

and reviewing if planning process and reducing conflict avoidance measures and education of major

shareholders. e.g. HMV music entertainment business major shareholders who must need to approve the

MAMA music entertainment Group major shareholders offer during their communication must be needed to

involve in their every time board of meeting in decision making process, project team needs to support staffs,

giving negotiation, reducing threatening where there is still restrain to them.

Q3 Analyze two driving forces and two restraining forces which are influencing HMV's

transformation plan as it tries to change the direction of the organization.

Driving forces which are influencing it (HMV company) tries to change the direction of organization successfully include: falling sales and growth of illegal download is existing in music entertainment market, which may make internal stakeholders more willing to co-operate, as well as management enthusiasm is for expanding into live music as a new marker. These is external and internal factors support to achieve takeover planning is successfully.

Restraining forces which are influencing it (HMV company) tries to takeover MAMA Group to change direction of organization successfully. HMV company may not be recognized as player in the live music market because it lacks management expertise in the cinema market and artist areas and MAMA Group which is focus on these market areas, instead of music area; HMV's takeover offer for MAMA Group is subject to approval from shareholders, who are concerned about HMV moving into a market where it has limited direct experience, along with prospects of raising finance to fund the takeover. This contrasts with the enthusiastic view of HMV's management who are keen to explore the prospects of live music as a new market. These are external and internal factors threat to implement takeover planning successfully.

Q4 Using an appropriate businesses model, analyse how HMV's proposed takeover of the MAMA Group will give it a competitive advantage in the music industry.

Entertainment music firm HMV is expanding its presence in the live music market by buying venue owner

MAMA Group for $46 million. MAMA group runs concert venues including the Hammersmith Apollo in

London. MAMA Group also owns other interests, e.g. an artist management business representing,

artic monkeys etc vaccines business areas.

A force field business model should be constructed with driving and restraining forces identified on

opposing sides in columns to the left and right of a centrally recognised proposal for HMV Group change

to takeover of HAMA Group in music industry.

Each force should have on estimated score noted beside it (1 is the most weak to 5 is the most strong) and these

should be totalled at the bottom of each column. Thus, the questionnaires can analyze how HMV proposed

takeover of MAMA Group will give it a competitive advantage in music market.

HMV music entertainment company needs for a new area of operation to compensate for problems in

traditional areas in music industry.

The Driving forces factors estimated score is needed for change include that it needs enthusiasm of

management, wider market (spreads operational risk), improving profitability aim every year, accessing

to new expertise in MAMA group etc factors.

The restraining forces against factors estimated score for change is who the shareholders need spend

too much cost to approve the takeover include that HMV and MAMA Groups are two different music

company. They have differences in corporate cultures need to adapt if HAMA Group wanted takeover

MAMA Group, it is possible that there is potential staff redundancies change occurrence etc factors.

These are HMV Group external and internal factors to analyse how HMV's proposed takeover of the

MAMA Group will give it a competitive advantage in the music industry.

CHAPTER XII

Explaining international trading management strategies

Q1 Define the term globalisation

Globalization means integration of world economies through free trade, free flow of capital and cheaper

foreign labour markets. The free trade of goods, capital ad labour in worldwide markets. It is

unrestricted by trade barriers, such as tariffs.

On the global stage, competitive advantages are gained by creating, transferring and exploiting competences

across operations and locations internationally.

Economic effects of globalization include global economic growth and distribution.

Globalization results multinational organizations are heavily involved in global changes. Many of these

organizations are pursuing joint ventures with firms from other countries.

Q2 Explain two potential advantages to Kraft of taking over Cadbury

Takeover means one business, usually larger one, buys controlling interest of another business.

Kraft is USA one chocolate and cheese and cake foods sale company, it takes over Cadbury UK chocolate

company potential advantages include that instant growth to enter European chocolate market in short term;

increasing geographic and chocolate markets expanding to European market spread; acquired European chocolate manufacturing local experts skills and European supply chain contacts to suppliers more easier;

acquisition may be at lower than the chocolate market value of the assets if the acquired business is in

difficulty.

Q3 Analyze the problems Kraft might experience as it tries to enter the European chocolate market.

Kraft is one USA chocolate, cheese and cake foods sale company, it tries to enter the European chocolate

market, it might experience these problems.

It can lack to understand of European local culture to known European clients chocolate taste, it can lack

ability to contract and supply a distribution chains to enter European chocolate easily, A lot of

European who don't accept to eat America brand chocolate, cheese and cake foods easily,

Kraft's American staffs will feel difficult to speak European language to work in European, Kraft's

American staffs need to adapt time difference to work in European, different European consumer law

regards chocolate, cheese and cake foods product content, spending advertising to attract European

consumers.

Q4 Discuss how Ansoff's matrix model might have been useful to Kraft in making the decision

to take over Cadbury.

Ansoff's matrix can make the decision to help Kraft to take over Cadbury in chocolate market.

It can help it's business to analyze how to expand market growth and product growth strategies, it provides a formal basis for logical and systematic analysis to that all options are considered and

Kraft can encourage consideration of alternative strategic options.

Kraft might have these business strategies in making the decision to take over Cadbury.

Market penetration strategy means existing products in existing markets. Although, this strategy has no applicable to Kraft because Kraft has no it's USA brand chocolates to exist presence in the European chocolate market.

However, after it takes over Cadbury in European chocolate market successfully, it can increase it Kraft chocolate numbers to European largely. It is low risk strategy, may be achieved by improving Kraft and Cadbury chocolate product element mix, promotion can be forced on future European existing clients to make more purchase.

Market development strategy means existing products enter to new markets. Kraft may see opportunity to reposition some existing European Cadbury brands chocolate foods to sell to new chocolate market.

For example: Asian countries include Hong Kong, Taiwan, China, Japan etc. It is medium risk strategy, it can be risky if have little knowledge of the new market, Kraft needs new distribution channels to sell these Asian countries new chocolate markets.

Product development strategy means new products enter new markets. Kraft and Cadbury brand chocolates may to renew to resign their package design and may give discount to pricing to be adapted to these Asian countries new chocolate market. It is medium risk strategy, it may be suitable if Kraft and Cadbury chocolate food products have reached saturation or decline. It is a reason why Kraft acquires Cadbury chocolate business.

Diversification means new products enter in new markets. It is high risk strategy, it can gain market share in existing markets, it is spread risk and it is often a reason why businesses acquire new businesses.

For example, Kraft and Cadbury co-operate to produce new taste of chocolates, cheeses and cake foods to sell to Asia countries, e.g. China, Hong Kong , Japan, Korean etc countries.

www.ingramcontent.com/pod-product-compliance
Ingram Content Group UK Ltd.
Pitfield, Milton Keynes, MK11 3LW, UK
UKHW041843200726
13854UKWH00005BA/2045

9 798888 050712